HEIGHT

Chris Woodford

Gareth Stevens
Publishing

Please visit our website, www.garethstevens.com. For a free color catalog of all our high-quality books, call toll-free 1-800-542-2595 or fax 1-877-542-2596.

Library of Congress Cataloging-in-Publication Data

Woodford, Chris.
Height / Chris Woodford.
    p. cm. — (Measure up math)
Includes index.
ISBN 978-1-4339-7442-7 (pbk.)
ISBN 978-1-4339-7443-4 (6-pack)
ISBN 978-1-4339-7441-0 (library binding)
1. Measurement—Juvenile literature. 2. Altitudes—Measurement—Juvenile literature. I. Title.
QA465.W654 2005
516'.15—dc23

2011045527

Published in 2013 by
Gareth Stevens Publishing
111 East 14th Street, Suite 349
New York, NY 10003

© 2013 Brown Bear Books Ltd

For Brown Bear Books Ltd:
Editorial Director: Lindsey Lowe
Managing Editor: Tim Harris
Children's Publisher: Anne O'Daly
Art Director: Jeni Child
Designer: Lynne Lennon
Picture Manager: Sophie Mortimer
Production Director: Alastair Gourlay

Picture Credits:
Key: t = top, tr = top right, b = bottom
Front Cover: Thinkstock: istockphoto
Interior: Shutterstock: 4–5, 5tr, 28b, Alhovik 6, 11, Galyna Andrushko 22–23, Goran Boicevic 27, Golden Pixels 7tr, Lasse Kristensen 28b, Francisco Leitao 23tr, Odua Images 17tr, Slavoljub Pantelic 9, Andrej Pol 20, Dave Pusey 8, Seregram 6l, Skobrik 10, John Wollwerth 15r; **Thinkstock:** Hemera 13tr, Stockbyte 16–17; **Topfoto:** Imagno 26.
All other artworks and photographs Brown Bear Books.
Brown Bear Books has made every attempt to contact the copyright holder. If anyone has any information could they please contact smortimer@windmillbooks.co.uk

All Artworks © Brown Bear Books Ltd

Publisher's note to educators and parents: Our editors have carefully reviewed the websites that appear on p. 31 to ensure that they are suitable for students. Many websites change frequently, however, and we cannot guarantee that a site's future contents will continue to meet our high standards of quality and educational value. Be advised that students should be closely supervised whenever they access the Internet.

Manufactured in the United States of America
1 2 3 4 5 6 7 8 9   12 11 10

CPSIA compliance information: Batch #BRS12GS: For further information contact Gareth Stevens, New York, New York at 1-800-542-2595.

CONTENTS

WHAT IS HEIGHT?

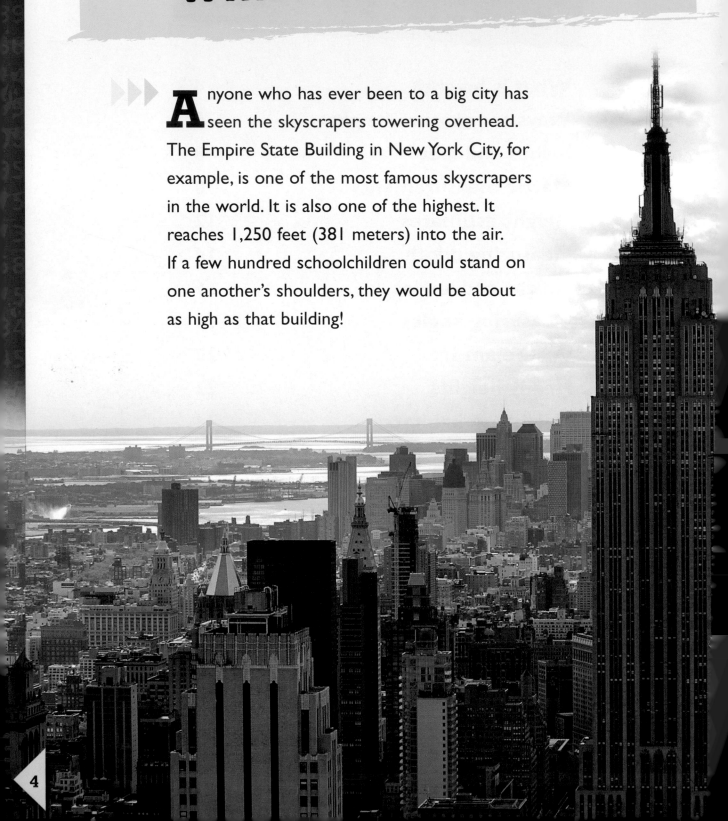

▶▶▶ **A**nyone who has ever been to a big city has seen the skyscrapers towering overhead. The Empire State Building in New York City, for example, is one of the most famous skyscrapers in the world. It is also one of the highest. It reaches 1,250 feet (381 meters) into the air. If a few hundred schoolchildren could stand on one another's shoulders, they would be about as high as that building!

People are a tiny bit taller when they wake in the morning than when they go to bed at night. During the day, a person's weight squeezes the body downward. It squashes the bones in a person's back so they take up less room. When someone lies in bed, the bones stretch out again.

▲ **When you go to sleep, your body relaxes and even gets a tiny bit taller!**

◀ **The Empire State Building is 1,250 feet (381 meters) tall.**

FACT

330 children, standing one on top of another, would reach the top of the Empire State Building!

Height and length

Height is a measurement. It is just like distance. The height of the Empire State Building is how far it goes up in the air.

Length is a measurement along the ground. Measuring length is the same as measuring distance. Suppose we could lay the Empire State Building on its side. Then we could measure its height by measuring how long it stretched down the street. So measuring height is really the same as measuring length or distance.

WORD BANK   *Distance: the length of the space between two places*

WAYS TO MEASURE HEIGHT

▶▶▶ **W**e can measure shorter distances with a ruler or a tape measure. We can measure height just the same as we measure length. But we have to use the ruler pointing upward instead of lying flat or sideways.

Rulers and tape measures

Rulers and tape measures come in different lengths. A school ruler is usually about 1 foot, or 12 inches (30 centimeters), long.

FACT

The longest tape measure you can buy in a hardware store is 300 feet long.

◀ **A school ruler (far left) cannot measure as far as a tape measure.**

HOW TO MEASURE YOUR HEIGHT

**Stand against a wall and put a book flat
on top of your head. Turn around but
keep the book in place. Make a small
pencil mark on the wall just under the
book. Ask an adult's permission first!
Now use a ruler or tape to measure the
distance from the pencil mark to the
ground. That measurement is your height.**

▶ **Make sure your heels touch the wall
when you measure height like this.**

+ − = x + − = x + − = x + − = x + − = + − = x + − = x + − =

A yardstick is 3 feet, or 36 inches (91 centimeters)
long. For measuring longer distances, we have to use
a tape measure. Tape measures can be any length
from a few feet to hundreds of feet. Sometimes tape
measures wrap onto a reel with a handle to make
them easier to use.

Rulers and tape measures have lines marked along
the side to show measurements. These lines are
called the scale.

WORD BANK   *Scale: the marks and numbers on the side of a ruler*

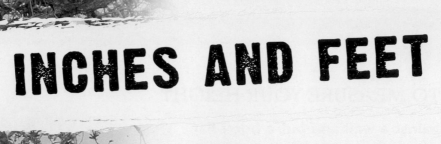

INCHES AND FEET

When we use a ruler or tape measure, we usually read height in yards, feet, or inches. We could use a ruler and find that a small bird is about 6 inches high. With a tape measure, we might find an adult is 6 feet tall. If we stood on a ladder, we could measure the height of a house. We might find it was 6 yards high.

◀ A giraffe is hundreds of times taller than a fly or an earthworm.

▶ HOW HIGH IS THAT?

Different animals have very different heights. Here are the average heights of some common animals, plus a giraffe:

Fly..................... ¼ inch
Earthworm......... ¼ inch
Lizard............... 1 to 2 inches
Cat.................... 1 foot
Dog...................6 inches to 3 feet
Human..............5 to 6 feet
Horse .... 5 to 7 feet
Giraffe.............. 15 to 19 feet

Units are important

The house, the person, and the bird all measure six units. But the house is taller than the person, who is much taller than the bird. The number six means something different each time.

We call yards, feet, and inches the units of measurement. A unit is part of a measurement. It tells how big the measurement is. A yard is bigger than a foot, and a foot is bigger than an inch.

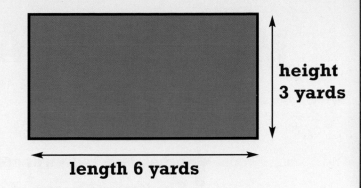

height x length = area

6 yards x 3 yards = 18 square yards

Area of the wall = 18 square yards

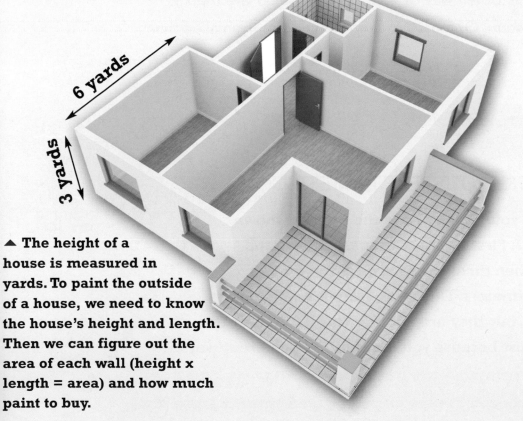

▲ The height of a house is measured in yards. To paint the outside of a house, we need to know the house's height and length. Then we can figure out the area of each wall (height x length = area) and how much paint to buy.

METRIC MEASUREMENTS

Inches, feet, and yards are called imperial units. The imperial system of measurement is the commonly used system in the United States. In other parts of the world, people commonly measure heights with different units. These units include millimeters, centimeters, and meters.

This other way of measuring is called the metric system. One metric centimeter (cm) is smaller than

▶ **TRY THIS** + – = x + – = x + – = x

MEASURE YOURSELF IN METRIC

Measure your height using the method shown on page 7. First measure yourself in feet and inches. Then measure your height in meters and centimeters. The measurements will look different, but they are not. Your height does not change just because you measure it in different ways.

half an inch. There are 2.54 cm in 1 inch.
A hundred centimeters make 1 meter (m).
And a thousand meters make 1 kilometer (km).

Metric rulers and tape measures

Rulers and tapes are marked with either imperial
or metric units. Sometimes a ruler has inches down
one side and centimeters down the other.

▶ CHANGING HEIGHTS

If 4 feet are the same as 1.2
meters, 8 feet must be the
same as 2.4 meters. We can
always change feet and inches
into meters and centimeters.
The table at right gives some
height measurements in both
imperial and metric units.

1 inch (2.54 cm)

- 1 inch is the same as 2.54 centimeters
- 1 foot, or 12 inches, is the same as 30 centimeters
- 1 centimeter is the same as 0.4 inch, or $^2/_5$ inch
- 1 meter, or 100 centimeters, is the same as 3 feet 3 inches, or 39 inches

Metric scale

Imperial scale

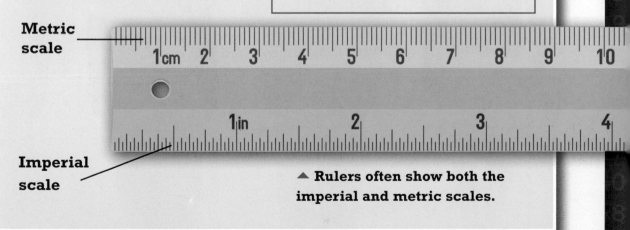

▲ Rulers often show both the imperial and metric scales.

HEIGHT ESTIMATES

▶▶▶ **W**hen a person finds something's height with a ruler, that is called a measurement. A measurement is usually very careful and exact. But we do not always have to measure something to find its height. Sometimes we can figure it out

▼ If you know how tall one person is, you can estimate the height of the others by comparing them to that person.

**4 feet 3 inches
(1.3 meters)**

▶ GOOD ESTIMATES

Say you estimate the height of a dog and then measure it. If your estimate was close to the measurement, that was a good estimate. If your estimate was a long way off, it was a bad estimate. An estimate is different from a guess. With an estimate, we want to be as accurate as possible. With a guess, accuracy does not matter.

▲ If you know how tall the big dog is, it is easier for you to estimate the height of the small dog.

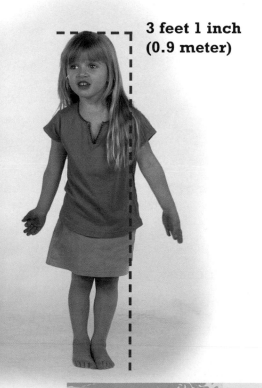

3 feet 1 inch (0.9 meter)

just by looking. That measurement is called an estimate because it is not exact. If you know that you are about 4 feet 3 inches (1.3 meters) tall, you can probably guess how tall your friends are. Some will be taller, but your little sister will be shorter.

It is easiest to estimate the height of something if you have measured something else first. Suppose you have measured the height of a cat. Now suppose a dog stands beside it. You can probably estimate the height of the dog quite easily. But if you had not measured the cat, it would not be so easy.

WORD BANK   *Estimate: a rough calculation, better than a guess*

MEASURING DEPTH

Buildings and people have height because they stand up above the ground. There is also another kind of height that goes down, sometimes deep underground. That measurement is depth. For example, water can be deep. A swimming pool may be 3 to 6 feet (1 to 3 meters) deep. The ocean is much deeper than this. The farther out someone goes from the shore, the deeper the water gets.

▲ Divers use special equipment called scuba-diving gear so that they can breathe underwater. With no scuba gear, a person can only dive down to about 100 feet (30 meters).

INTO THE DEEP

The world's oceans are not the same depth all over. The deepest part of all the oceans is a place called the Mariana Trench, which is in the Pacific Ocean south of Japan.

The Mariana Trench is 7 miles (11 kilometers) deep. If that distance was laid in a straight line along the ground, it would take about two hours to walk from one end to the other!

▲ Swimming pools are usually not very deep. Most are no more than 6 feet 6 inches (2 meters) deep.

Measuring depth

People measure the depth of the ocean in different ways. Sometimes they lower measuring ropes over the side of a ship. These ropes have weights tied to them to make them sink. People can also use sound to measure the ocean depth. They send a beam of sound down from a ship. Then they time how long it takes for the sound to bounce back up off the ocean floor. That tells them how deep the water is.

WORD BANK   *Scuba gear: air tank, face mask, wet suit, and flippers*

HEIGHT AND ANGLES

▶▶▶ **I**f you stand up straight against a wall, you are at your full height. But if you stand a little distance away from the wall and lean back to touch it, your body will not reach up the wall so far, and you will not reach so high. The more you lean, the less high up the wall you reach. Try it and see!

When one thing leans against another, it makes an angle. An angle is the space between two lines that cross or meet. A small angle means there is not much space between the lines. A big angle means there is a lot of space between the lines.

▼ **The more you lean against a wall, the less high up the wall you reach and the bigger the angle you make.**

wall — height reached — right angle

wall — height reached — bigger angle

difference in height — wall — height reached — even bigger angle

+ – = x + – = x

RIGHT ANGLES

A square corner is a special kind of angle. When two lines meet so that they make a box-like corner, we call this a right angle. A right angle is like one corner of a square. Many of the things around us are made with right angles.

◆ **Look carefully at these pictures. How many right angles, or corners, can you see in the chair and the climbing bars?**

+ – = x + – = x

FACT

The legs of a chair are usually parallel to each other. So are the legs of a table.

MEASURING ANGLES

The measurements we make with a ruler are usually in inches. So a ruler's scale is marked with inches. But we do not measure angles in inches. Instead, angles have their own units called degrees. Degrees are measured with a protractor.

▶ Using a protractor, can you measure the two angles that have been marked in the picture?

▶ **TRY THIS**

+ – = x + – = x + – = x + – = x + – = + – =

USING A PROTRACTOR

A protractor has a target mark at the center of its bottom edge. To measure an angle, put the target mark on the point where the two lines meet. Line up the protractor so one of the lines runs along the protractor's zero line. Then you see where the other line meets the scale. Read the angle on the scale. Practice on the angles on the climbing frame photograph at right.

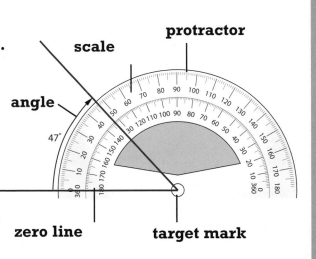

protractor

scale

angle

47°

zero line

target mark

+ – = x + – = x + – = x + – = x + – = + – = x + – = x+ – =

18

A protractor is like a curved ruler. Instead of measuring inches, it measures degrees.

To make an angle, two lines must cross or meet. We can draw lines at different angles to one another. The bigger the angle, the farther apart the lines are. Two lines drawn at 90 degrees or 90° make a square corner (right angle). The symbol ° is a quick way to write degrees. At an angle of 180 degrees, the two lines form a straight line.

WHERE AM I?

Finding out where in the world you are is called navigation. Modern ships navigate in many different ways. Before modern methods were invented, it was much harder for sailors to know where they were. Sailors often found their way by using the stars in the sky.

Sextants

Sailors could measure their position using a sextant. This instrument was first used in the 1730s. A sextant is like a small telescope fixed to a protractor. Sailors use sextants to measure the angle of the sun, the moon,

◀ **This sailor is using a sextant to figure out where he is. It is safe to look at the sun through a sextant. You should never look directly at the sun otherwise, though.**

The curved edge of a quadrant is divided into 0 to 90 degrees. A small weight, or plumb bob, is attached to the corner.

A sailor holds the quadrant so the plumb line falls across the degree scale. Then he or she looks along the straight edge until a star or the moon is in line with the sights. The angle is then read. Using this angle and the time of the day, the sailor can work out how far north or south of the equator the boat is.

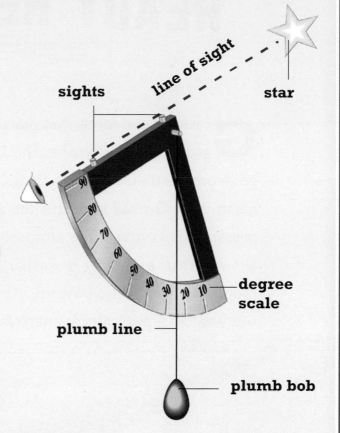

sights

line of sight

star

90 80 70 60 50 40 30 20 10

degree scale

plumb line

plumb bob

or a star above the horizon. This is a type of height measurement. With this angle, sailors can figure out how far north or south they are from the equator, as long as they also know the time of day.

Although sextants were invented hundreds of years ago, sailors still use them today alongside more modern methods.

WORD BANK   *Equator: the imaginary line that runs around Earth's center*

HEADY HEIGHTS

►►► **G**ravity is the force that pulls things toward the ground. It gets weaker the farther away you get from Earth. One of the things gravity pulls toward Earth is air. Gravity squeezes the air and makes air pressure. That makes the atmosphere, which is the air we breathe. Gravity is weaker at the top of a mountain than at the bottom. At the mountaintop, the weaker gravity means there is less air pressure.

► As you climb higher and higher up a mountain, the air pressure gets lower.

An airplane's height above Earth is called its altitude. Pilots need to know the altitude to help them fly the plane. They measure the airplane's height with an instrument in the plane called an altimeter. It works by measuring the air pressure. Then it changes this measurement to altitude.

▲ An airplane's control panel always includes an altimeter.

Climbing higher

Lack of air pressure makes it much harder to breathe than at the bottom of the mountain. The higher up you go, the lower the air pressure becomes. Scientific instruments that measure air pressure are called barometers. If we measure air pressure with a barometer, we can use it to find out how high up we are. The air pressure can be useful for measuring the height of a mountain.

WORD BANK *Atmosphere: the gases (air) that are around Earth*

HEIGHTS OF HABITATS

▶▶▶ **T**here are millions of different types of animals living on Earth. Each species, or type, of animal is best suited to living in a particular type of place. The type of place an animal lives is called its habitat. A polar bear's habitat is the frozen Arctic. An alligator's habitat is a freshwater swamp or river.

Heights and depths

For many animals, height or depth is an important feature of their habitat. In a rainforest, for example, different types of animals live at different heights.

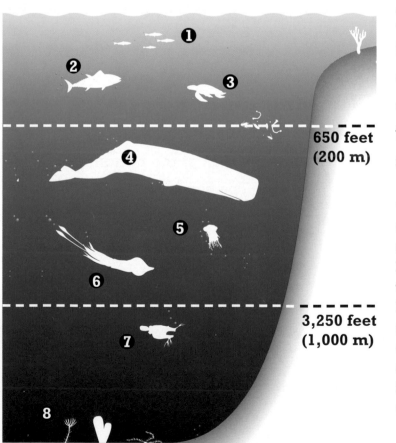

650 feet (200 m)

3,250 feet (1,000 m)

◀ The deeper the water, the darker it gets. Different animals are best suited to each layer. Herring (1), tuna (2), and sea turtles (3) live in the sunny top layer of the ocean. Sperm whales (4) and jellyfish (5) live in deeper, darker waters. Giant squid (6) and deep-sea anglerfish (7) stay in the depths. Sponges and brittle stars (8) live on the seafloor.

Rainforest trees can be more than 200 feet (61 meters) high. A few giant trees grow even taller. Trees in a rainforest make layers, like the stories of a building. The top branches get lots of sun. The layers get darker farther down. Different animals live in each layer.

▶ RAINFOREST LAYERS

Canopy
The treetops form a crowded, leafy roof called the canopy. Many birds, climbing animals, and insects live in the canopy.

- -

Understory
The understory is shaded from the sun by the canopy. Butterflies, snakes, and anteaters called tamanduas live in the understory.

- -

Forest floor
Little light reaches the forest floor. Jaguars, warthogs, peccaries, and other animals live down here.

WORD BANK *Understory: plants that grow in the lowest part of the forest*

RECORD BREAKERS

We can find out some amazing things by measuring heights. If no one ever measured heights, we would never know the height of the world's tallest man. He was named Robert Pershing Wadlow and he lived from 1918 to 1940. When he was last measured, he had grown to the height of 8 feet 11 inches (2 meters and 72 centimeters)!

Dogs and horses

Other animals can also reach amazing heights. One of the world's tallest breeds of dog is called the Great Dane. A Great Dane usually grows to a height of nearly 3 feet (91 centimeters). That is taller than

◀ **Robert Pershing Wadlow with his brothers. In this picture, he was almost fully grown.**

a lot of young children. A Great Dane called George was 43 inches (1 meter and 9 centimeters) tall in 2011. Horses can also be very tall. Many horses grow to heights of 6 to 7 feet (1.8 to 2.1 meters).

▶ The Burj Khalifa in Dubai became the world's tallest building when it was completed in 2010. It is 2,717 feet (828 meters) tall.

▶ TALLEST BUILDINGS

Listed here are some of the tallest buildings in the world. Each one is the same height as hundreds of 6-foot (1.8 meter) adults standing on one another's shoulders.

Tall building	How high is it?	How many people tall?
KVLY-TV mast, North Dakota, USA	2,063 feet (629 meters)	344 people
CN Tower, Toronto, Canada	1,815 feet (553 meters)	303 people
Taipei 101 skyscraper, Taiwan	1,667 feet (508 meters)	278 people

WORD BANK   *Mast: a very narrow vertical structure*

ESTIMATING HEIGHTS

YOU WILL NEED

- **A ruler or tape measure**
- **A pencil and paper**
- **A piece of chalk**
- **Three or four friends or family members to help you**

WHAT TO DO

1. Ask one friend to stand straight against a wall. Mark where the top of his or her head is on the wall with the chalk. Be careful not to damage the wall. Ask someone's permission first.

2. Measure down from the mark to the ground. Write down the height on paper.

3. Now you can measure your other friends or people in your family. Look at each person and think about their heights. Are they taller or shorter than the person you just measured? How much taller or shorter?

4. Estimate each person's height. Write down what you think each person's height is.

5. Now measure their heights just as you did for the first person. Write the heights down next to your estimates.

6. Were your estimates close? You should find that you get better and better at estimating as you go along.

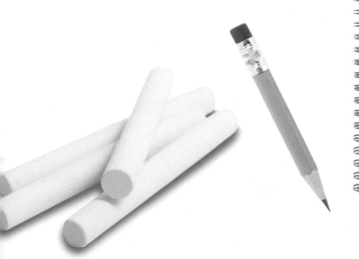

Always write down the units!

When you write down your measurement, always write the units as well as the number. Your ruler or tape measure may be in inches, feet, centimeters, or meters. Make sure you write the unit as well as the number, so write 6 inches or 6 centimeters, not just 6.

GLOSSARY

altimeter A device in an airplane that measures height.

altitude Height above sea level.

angle The space between two lines that cross or meet.

atmosphere The gases (air) we breathe that surround Earth.

centimeter A small distance equal to one meter divided by 100.

degree A unit for measuring angles.

depth Height that goes downward.

distance A measurement of the space between two points.

equator The imaginary line that runs around Earth's center.

estimate A rough calculation, better than a guess.

foot An imperial distance equal to 12 inches (or 30 centimeters).

gravity A force that pulls things toward Earth.

height A distance between two points, measured upward.

imperial The commonly used system of measurements in the United States. The imperial system is based on inches, feet, and yards.

inch An imperial distance, which is the same as 2.54 centimeters in the metric system.

length A distance measured sideways or along the ground.

mast A very thin vertical structure.

meter A metric measurement equal to 3 feet 3 inches.

metric A set of measurements based on the meter.

navigation A way of finding a position on Earth, at sea, or in space.

parallel A pair of lines that never meet or touch.

protractor A device for measuring angles.

right angle A 90-degree angle.

ruler A straight measuring tool.

scale The marks on the side of a ruler, tape measure, or protractor.

sextant An old-fashioned device used for navigating at sea.

scuba gear Air tank, face mask, wet suit, and flippers used for diving.

tape measure A long, flexible ruler.

yard An imperial distance equal to 3 feet, which is the same as 91 centimeters in the metric system.

FIND OUT MORE

BOOKS

Marcie Aboff, *The Tallest Snowman.* Minneapolis, MN: Picture Window, 2008.

Brian Cleary, *How Long or How Wide?* Minneapolis, MN: Millbrook, 2007.

Jerry Pallotta, *Weights and Measures.* New York, NY: Scholastic, 2008.

Victoria Parker, *How Tall Is Tall: Comparing Structures.* Chicago, IL: Heinemann Library, 2011.

Henry Pluckrose, *What Size Is It?* North Mankato, MN: Sea to Sea Publications, 2007.

WEBSITES

Metric conversion chart
Convert lengths from imperial to metric units and from metric to imperial.
http://www.sciencemadesimple.com/length_conversion.php

Johnnie's Math Page
Plenty of measurement puzzles designed to increase your measuring ability and speed.
http://jmathpage.com/JIMSMeasurementlengthmass
volume.html

INDEX